Birds of Devon

Trevor and Endymion Beer

Tor Mark Press • Redruth

The Tor Mark series

First published 1999 by Tor Mark Press
United Downs Industrial Estate, St Day, Redruth, Cornwall TR16 5HY

ISBN 0-85025-376-4

The upper photograph on page 5 is reproduced by courtesy of Alan Beaumont. All other photographs are by the authors.

Printed in Great Britain by R Booth (Troutbeck Press), Mabe, Penryn, Cornwall

A Dunnock feeding a young Cuckoo

Introduction

This book looks at some of the birds one would expect to find whilst exploring the Devon countryside by coast, estuary and inland along the lanes and in woodland. It is not intended as a detailed ornithological field guide. We have concentrated on species usually met with in spring and summer.

Species are arranged in the main habitat type they favour but it should be borne in mind that green woodpeckers visit coastal sites, for example, just as curlews may be found breeding on moorland and feeding at an estuary, depending on time of year.

Measurements given are from the tip of the bill to the tip of the tail. Identification details are for adult males and females.

Common owls and birds of prey are collected together at the end of the book for ease of reference.

Food quoted is for birds in the wild. Many of the species mentioned will come to bird tables and feeders in gardens and some nest in garden habitats.

Coast

Shag 30 in (75 cm)

Also known as Green Cormorant. Black plumage with glossy green tinge. No white patches. Distinct crest on head in spring and summer. Upright stance and rapid flight with neck held outstretched. Sexes look alike. Stays all year in coastal habitats where it also breeds. Resident and sedentary species rarely found away from the sea. Nests in colonies on cliffs, rocks and ledges. Feeds on fish.

Cormorant 36 in (90 cm)

Black with greenish gloss to feathers. White face patch and white patch on thighs in summer. Immatures may show larger white patches. Sexes look alike. Upright stance and powerful flight with neck held outstretched like a shag. Often seen perched with spread wings to dry feathers after diving for fish. Essentially a coastal and estuary bird, but often seen inland at reservoirs and lakes. Resident and common. Nests in colonies on cliff ledges and grassy headlands. Feeds on fish and occasionally crabs.

Razorbill 16 in (40cm)

Member of Auk family,
an expert diver and
swimmer. Heavy bill,
black underparts, white
wing stripe. In summer
a white line shows from
bill to eye (black head
and neck). In winter
throat and sides of neck
become white. Sexes
look alike. Upright
stance. Resident but
most birds move out to
sea in winter. Nests on
coastal cliff crevices or
under boulders. Feeds
on fish, shellfish and
worms.

Top: Cormorant

Below: Razorbill

Kittiwake

16 in (40 cm)

White gull with black wing-tips, uniform grey head and neck in winter. Black legs and yellow bill. Immatures have dark stripes on wings; dark markings on head in winter. Sexes look alike. Resident. Nests in colonies, usually on narrow cliff ledges, sometimes in sea caves. Feeds almost entirely on fish and fish offal. Has a 'gentle' look.

Guillemot

$16^1/2$ in (42 cm)

Similar to Razorbill, but has pronounced pointed bill and is dark brown rather than black. Greyer in winter and, as with Razorbill, has white underparts. A 'bridled' variety has a white eye ring with a white line extending back over sides of head. Upright stance. Sexes look alike. Resident. Winters at sea. Nests in

Far left: Kittiwake   Above left: Guillemot   Right: Herring Gull

colonies, usually near Razorbills and other sea birds. Feeds on fish, shellfish, worms and some seaweeds.

Herring Gull   23 in (57 cm)

Grey back, white underparts, yellow bill with red spot on lower mandible. Pink legs, dark wing-tips flecked with white. Young are brown-backed with a dark tail band. Sexes look alike. Resident and widespread inland and on estuaries. Nests in colonies on cliff ledges and increasingly on buildings. Feeds on fish, offal, eggs and chicks of other birds and shellfish. Has a 'fierce' appearance.

7

Black-headed Gull   15 in (37$^{1}/_{2}$ cm)

Chocolate-brown hood (lost in winter), grey back and wings, white neck and underparts. Black wing-tips. Red bill, legs and feet. Young are brown and white with brown band on tail-tip. Sexes look alike. Winter adult plumage includes dark smudge at ears. Resident. Nests in colonies. Feeds on scraps, offal, fish such as sand eels, crabs, snails, worms and insects.

Great Black-backed Gull   27 in (67 cm)

Black back, white underparts. Immatures are brown above, pale below. Legs pink. Sexes look alike. Resident. Nests in small groups on ground, cliff ledges and rocky stacks. Feeds on almost any animal food including dead fish, carrion, offal and other birds. Occasionally eats vegetable matter. Common on estuaries.

Fulmar   18$^{1}/_{2}$ in (46 cm)

Dark grey back, wings and tail. White head and underparts. 'Tubular' nostrils clearly visible at close range. Sexes look alike. Resident. Nests on cliffs on turf or depressions in rocks. Feeds on fish and marine mammal offal, fish and crustaceans.

Below: Black-headed Gull

Above: Great Black-backed Gull
Below: Fulmar

Shelduck   26 in (65 cm)

Black, white and chestnut plumage. Adults have a red bill (drakes have a knob at the base of the bill). Resident. Nests in bramble brakes, rabbit burrows and other well-concealed sites. Feeds on molluscs, crabs and shrimps, insects and vegetable matter. Common on estuary saltings. The largest British duck species.

Oystercatcher   17 in (42 cm)

Black and white plumage, long orange bill, pink legs. An unmistakable wader. Sexes look alike. Resident. Nests around the coast on cliffs, usually in grassy areas. Feeds on shellfish, crustaceans, crabs and shrimps, as well as worms and insects inland. Common on estuaries and around rocky coasts.

Ringed Plover $7^1/_2$ in (18 cm)

Black collar, and black and white head pattern. Greyish-brown above, white below. Yellow legs and short yellow bill with dark tip. Prominent wing-bar visible in flight. Sexes look alike. Resident. Nests in scrapes on turf or shingle beach. Feeds on insects, molluscs, crustaceans, worms and some vegetable matter. Often seen with other waders on estuaries.

Above left: Shelduck   Above: Oystercatcher
Below: Ringed Plover

Snipe   10 in (26 cm)

Brown streaked and patterned plumage. Long straight bill and boldly striped head. Zig-zag flight pattern. Usually utters a harsh call when disturbed into flight. Sexes look alike. Resident, but much commoner in winter. Nests in rushes, sedges and grasses in ground hollows near water in wild areas such as Exmoor and Dartmoor. Feeds on worms, beetles, snails, woodlice, grubs and caddis larvae as well as seeds of some marsh plants.

Lapwing   12 in (30 cm)

Also called Green Plover and Peewit. Black and white with rich greeny tinge on back. Rounded wings and short tail, head crest and long legs. Sexes look alike. Resident. Nests in ploughed fields, marshes and scrapes on the ground. Feeds on insects, such as leatherjackets, and on worms.

Curlew   22 in (55 cm)

The largest British wader. Rich grey-brown plumage and white rump, long legs and unmistakable long down-curved bill. Listen for distinctive 'coor-li' cry. Sexes look alike. Resident. Breeds on high moors, but likes estuaries where large numbers build up from late August to April. Nests in hollows amongst moorland vegetation. Feeds on molluscs, crustaceans, worms and small fish on coast; worms, molluscs, berries and seeds inland.

Above left: Snipe   *Above: Lapwing*
Below: Curlew

Dipper

On or near fresh water

Dipper   7 in (17¹/2 cm)

Dark brown plumage with strikingly white breast. Look for pronounced dipping and bobbing action when perched. Rarely away
from water. Sexes look alike. Resident. Nests on ledges or in cavities close to water. Feeds on water-beetles, caddis larvae and
nymphs of dragonflies and mayflies, worms, tadpoles and tiny
fish. Direct, fast flight.

Grey Wagtail   8 in (20 cm)

Blue-grey above, yellow below including tail feathers. Long
black tail with white sides. Male has black throat in summer,
white in winter. Female plumage more buff, generally less
colourful. Resident. Nests in crevices usually close to water, or
occasionally in old nests of dippers or other birds and on buildings. Feeds on many insect species and some molluscs.
Undulating flight.

Pied Wagtail   7 in (17 cm)

Black and white plumage, long tail wagged up and down whilst
perching. Undulating flight. Females have greyish back.
Resident. Nests in holes of banks and hedges, or in walls, sheds
and thatch. Often quite urban in its habitat choice. Feeds on
insects including flies, moths and beetles.

Above: Grey Wagtail
Below: Pied Wagtail

Grey Heron   36 in (90 cm)

Tall, upright grey bird with dark grey flight feathers and black crest on head. Pale below, and very long legs. Stout yellow dagger-like bill. Flies with head drawn in and legs trailing. Resident. Sexes look alike. Nests in colonies in trees, very occasionally in reedbeds. Feeds on fish, small mammals, beetles, frogs and rats.

Kingfisher $6^1/2$ in ($16^1/2$ cm)

Unmistakable with its brilliant blue-green plumage above and orange-chestnut below. Sexes look alike, except adult female shows orange on lower mandible (male's is black). Resident. Nests in tunnels hacked from river, stream or canal bank. Feeds on small fish plus some water insect life. Very fast direct flight.

Reed Bunting   6 in (15 cm)

Male has black head and throat, and white collar. In breeding season it has a dark brown streaked back and grey rump, and is greyish white below. Head pattern is obscured in winter. Female all brown, streaked and lighter below with black and white moustachial stripe. Resident. Nests in tussocks or on ground in vegetation. Feeds on mainly marsh plant seeds, some animal food, including freshwater snails, beetles and other insects.

Above left: Grey Heron   Above: Kingfisher
Below: Reed Bunting (male)

Open country

Stonechat   5in (13cm)

Rounded-looking bird. In summer the male has a black head and back, with white patches at neck, wings and rump, and a bright chestnut breast. Browner and duller in winter. Female has streaky brown upperparts in summer, darker in winter.

Nests on or close to ground, often at base of gorse bushes. Males hold territory from tops of shrubs. Resident. Feeds on insects and their larvae, some worms and spiders.

Skylark   7 in (17 cm)

Streaked brown bird with white outer tail feathers, a small head crest and whitish line along trailing edge of wings. Sexes look alike. Resident. Known best by characteristic soaring song flight. Makes cup nests of grass on ground, usually hidden well in grassy tussocks. Feeds on plant seeds and some leaves, including clover, worms, caterpillars and insects, spiders and other tiny ground animals. Some grain also taken.

Yellow Hammer   6 in (16 cm)

Also called Yellow Bunting. Male has bright yellow and chestnut plumage. Female is duller and more streaked with brown. Look for bright chestnut rump. Resident bird of open country with trees. Well known for the 'little bit of bread and no cheese' song. Nests in hedgerows and banks, on ground or in ivy on walls. Feeds largely on weed seeds, but also takes grain, wild fruit and insects.

Above: Skylark
Below: Yellowhammer

Above: Linnet
Below: Meadow Pipit

Linnet   5¹/₄ in (13 cm)

Chestnut, with white wing bar. Forked tail with white sides. Male has crimson crown and breast in summer. Resident. Nests close to ground in bushes. Feeds on weed seeds, and some insects, particularly caterpillars, are fed to the young.

Meadow Pipit   5³/₄ in (15 cm)

Olive-brown above with dark markings. Breast streaked with white; markings dense. Outer tail feathers white. Legs brownish. Long hind claw. Sexes look alike. Resident. Makes grass nests on ground. Feeds on insects mainly, with spiders, earthworms and seeds also taken.

Coastal woodland and cliffs

Jay   13¹/₂ in (34 cm)

Brownish-pink plumage and blue wing patches with black barring. Black and white crown feathers, white rump very visible in flight, and white patch on each wing. Tail black. Sexes look alike. Resident. Nests in bushes or trees, usually up to 20 ft (6 m). Feeds on acorns, eggs, young birds, insects and larvae, worms and mice.

Jackdaw

Jackdaw   13 in (33 cm)

Black with grey nape which gives a hooded effect. Silver eyes. Sexes look alike. Resident. Nests in trees, buildings, crevices or cliff caves, often in chimneys. Feeds on insects and larvae, grain and seeds, fruit, small animals, eggs and young of other birds, carrion, potatoes and food scraps.

Woodland

Great Spotted Woodpecker   9 in ($22^{1}/2$ cm)

Basically a black and white bird with usual upright woodpecker stance. Distinct white 'shoulder' patches, red undertail patches, white underparts. Cruciform black band on cheeks links to nape. Males have white forehead, black crown and red on nape. Females have entirely black crown. Resident. Nests in treeholes. Feeds on beetles and their larvae, nuts, conifer seeds and berries.

Goldfinch   5in (13cm)

Once called the seven-coloured finch. Velvety scarlet, black and white head, black and yellow wings, white rump and deeply forked black tail. Upper parts are white whilst the fawn coloured chest fades to a creamy white belly. Sexes alike. Resident. Nests in trees, often in old orchards. Feeds on seeds, some fruit, and insects. Flocks often forage in hedgerows in autumn and winter.

Right: Great Spotted Woodpecker
Below: Goldfinch

Green Woodpecker   12$^{1}/_{2}$ in (32 cm)

Green upperparts, yellow on back and rump. Underparts grey-ish-green. Sometimes indistinct brownish bars show on belly and flanks. Crown is red in both sexes. Moustachial stripe is usually red in males and black in females. Resident. Nests in tree holes. Feeds on ants and their pupae, and other insects. Occasionally takes acorns, apples, grain and berries.

Nuthatch 5¹/₂in (14cm)

Slate blue-grey upper-parts, pinkish-buff below. Pronounced black eye stripe reaches nape. Stocky build and powerful chisel-shaped bill. Will climb down tree head first. Sexes look alike. Resident. Nests in tree holes and sometimes in hollow trees. Feeds on seeds, nuts, acorns and some insects and spiders.

Treecreeper 5in (12¹/₂cm)

Brown streaked upper-parts, silvery white beneath. Pale eyestripe, narrow down-curled bill. May climb trees in spiral fashion using its tail as a support (as woodpeckers do). Sexes look alike. Resident. Nests in bark crevices on tree trunks or old stumps, or in similar sites on buildings. Feeds on insects, woodlice, earwigs, cater-pillars and other small invertebrates, and on grain and seeds.

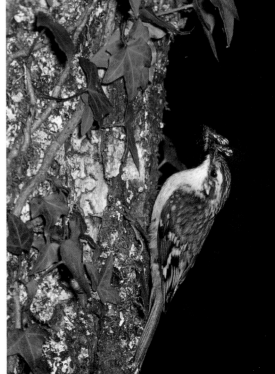

Song Thrush   9 in (22^1/$_2$ cm)

Brown upperparts. Breast buff, heavily streaked with chestnut and shading into white. Sexes look alike. Resident. Nests in bushes, hedgerows, trees and on ledges. Feeds on snails, worms, insects and larvae, fruit and seeds.

Mistle Thrush   10^1/$_2$ in (27 cm)

Grey-brown upperparts, very pale beneath with roundish chestnut spots, bolder than those of Song Thrush. White outer tail feathers. White undersides to wings. Sexes look alike. Resident. Nests mainly in woodlands, in trees. Feeds on insects and their larvae, spiders, snails, worms, fruit and berries.

Blackcap   5^1/$_2$ in (13^1/$_2$ cm)

Greyish upperparts. Ash grey cheeks and underparts. Males have pronounced black crown. Females have a chestnut brown 'cap' and somewhat browner underparts. Legs and beak dark. Summer visitor, April to September. Some wintering birds seen. Feeds on insects and berries.

Above left: Song Thrush Above right: Mistle Thrush
Below: Blackcap

Spotted Flycatcher   5¹/₂ in (13¹/₂ cm)

Grey-brown plumage. Small streaks on forehead and crown, and pale streaks on the off-white breast. Body appears long, with short legs. Sexes look alike. Summer visitor. Nests in trees, cavities, on ledges or behind creeper on walls, and occasionally in old birds' nests. Feeds almost entirely on flying insects, but may take earthworms and berries, particularly when insects are in short supply.

Pied Flycatcher

5 in (12^1/$_2$ cm)

Male black above with white forehead. White below with white wing bar. Female olive-brown upperparts, whitish-beige below, with smaller white patches on wings. Summer visitor. Nests in tree holes. Feeds mainly on insects, larvae and grubs, and occasionally takes worms.

Long Tailed Tit

5^1/$_2$ in (13^1/$_2$ cm)

Pink, black and white plumage. Black and white tail longer than body. Sexes look alike. Resident. Nests in intricate domed structure built into a bush or tree. Feeds mainly on insects and spiders, and occasionally on seeds and buds.

Birds of prey

Kestrel

$13^{1}/2$in (34cm)

Long narrow wings, long tail and noted for hovering flight. Male brick red with small dark spots, and grey crown, neck, ear patches, rump and tail. Underparts yellowish-brown with blackish streaks. Black band at end of tail which has a white tip. Narrow moustachial stripe. Females browner at head, tail with dark bars and less distinctive moustachial streak. Resident. Nests in old nests of crows, hollow trees, quarries and buildings.

Kestrels feed mainly on small rodents, insects, some small birds, frogs and lizards, and occasionally take worms.

Buzzard
Male 20 in (50 cm)
Female 23 in (57 1/2 cm)
Plumage dark brown
with lighter underparts.
Blackish beak, yellow
legs and feet. Dark eyes.
Soars over wooded
country: splays primaries
(like spread fingers).
Resident. Nests high in
trees, occasionally on
quarry and cliff ledges.
Feeds on rodents, other
mammals including
rabbits; some frogs,
snakes, earthworms and
beetles are also taken.

Sparrowhawk
Male 11 in (27 1/2 cm)
Female 15 in (37 1/2 cm)
Short, rounded wings
and long tail. Blue-grey
beak, bright yellow legs
and feet, and yellow
eyes. Male usually slate
grey above, reddish,
barred below, and some-
times has orangey eyes.
Female browner above,
darker brown under-
parts and white stripe
over eyes. Resident.
Nests in trees. Feeds on
small birds and rodents,
and a few insects.

Tawny Owl
15in (37$\frac{1}{2}$ cm)

Streaked and speckled grey-brown to red-brown plumage. Large rounded head, facial disc and dark eyes. Underparts may be grey-brown to beige with dark striations. Shortish, rounded wings show in flight. Resident. Nests in hollow trees, etc. Feeds on rats, mice and other mammals, birds, frogs, fish and insects.

Barn Owl
13$\frac{1}{2}$ in (34 cm)

Golden buff and pearl-grey plumage, finely spotted with white on upperparts. White 'disc' face, white underparts and feathery legs give a ghostly appearance. Deeply sunken dark eyes and long legs with black talons. Females may be slightly greyer. Resident. Nests in barns, hollow trees, quarries, etc. Feeds on mammals, small birds, insects and frogs.